ON THE IMPERIAL HIGHWAY

Other Books by Jayne Cortez

Pisstained Stairs and the Monkey Man's Wares

Festivals & Funerals

Scarifications

Mouth on Paper

Merveilleux Coup de Foudre: Poetry of Jayne Cortez and Ted Joans

Firespitter

Coagulations: New and Selected Poems

Poetic Magnetic

Fragments: Poetry of Jayne Cortez and the Sculpture of Melvin Edwards

Somewhere in Advance of Nowhere

Jazz Fan Looks Back

The Beautiful Book

Recordings (with music)

Celebrations and Solitudes

Unsubmissive Blues

There It Is

Maintain Control

Everywhere Drums

Cheerful & Optimistic

Taking the Blues Back Home

Borders of Disorderly Time

Find Your Own Voice

ON THE IMPERIAL HIGHWAY: NEW AND SELECTED POEMS

BY

JAYNE CORTEZ

Hanging Loose Press
Brooklyn, New York

Published by Hanging Loose Press, 231 Wyckoff Street, Brooklyn, New York 11217-2208.

www.hangingloosepress.com

Printed in the United States of America
10 9 8 7 6 5 4 3 2

Hanging Loose Press thanks the Literature Program of New York State Council on the Arts for a grant in support of the publication of this book.

Some of the poems in this collection were developed during my 2006 residency at Bellagio Study and Conference Center in Bellagio, Italy.

Cover art by Melvin Edwards
Cover design by Marie Carter

Library of Congress Cataloging-in-Publication Data available on request.

ISBN: 978-1-931236-90-4 (pbk.)
978-1-931236-99-7 (cloth)

TABLE OF CONTENTS

From *Somewhere in Advance of Nowhere* (1996)

From *The Beautiful Book* (2007)

What a Mouthfull

FROM *SCARIFICATIONS*

(1973)

I AM NEW YORK CITY

i am new york city
here is my brain of hot sauce
my tobacco teeth my
  mattress of bedbug tongue
legs apart hand on chin
  war on the roof insults
pointed fingers pushcarts
my contraceptives all

look at my pelvis blushing

i am new york city of blood
police and fried pies
i rub my docks red with grenadine
and jelly madness in a flow of tokay
my huge skull of pigeons
my séance of peeping toms
my plaited ovaries excuse me
this is my grime my thigh of
steelspoons and toothpicks
  i imitate no one

i am new york city
of the brown spit and soft tomatoes
give me my confetti of flesh
  my marquee of false nipples
my sideshow of open beaks
  in my nose of soot
in my ox bled eyes
in my ear of saturday night specials
i eat ha ha hee hee and ho ho

i am new york city
never-change-never-sleep-never-melt
  my shoes are incognito
cadavers grow from my goatee
look i sparkle with shit with wishbones
my nickname is glue-me

Take my face of stink bombs
my star spangled banner of hot dogs
take my beer can junta
my reptilian ass of footprints
and approach me through life
approach me through death
approach me through my widow's peak
through my split ends my
asthmatic laugh   approach me
through my wash rag
half ankle   half elbow
massage me with your camphor tears
  salute the patina and concrete
of my rat tail wig
  face up   face down   piss
into the bite of our handshake

i am new york city
my skillet-head friend
  my fat-bellied comrade
citizens
  break wind with me

DO YOU THINK

Do you think this is a sad day
  a sad night
full of tequila full of el dorado
  full of banana solitudes

And my chorizo face a holiday for knives
  and my arching lips a savannah for cuchifritos
and my spit curls a symbol for you
  to overcharge overbill oversell me
these saints these candles
  these dented cars loud pipes
no insurance and no place to park
  because my last name is Cortez

Do you think this is a sad night
  a sad day

And on this elevator
  between my rubber shoes
in the crème de menthe of my youth
  the silver tooth of my age
the gullah speech of my one trembling tit
full of tequila full of el dorado
  full of banana solitudes you say
i use more lights more gas
  more telephones more sequins more feathers
more iridescent head-stones
  you think i accept this pentecostal church
in exchange for everything stolen

And because my name is Cortez
  do you think this is a revision
of flesh studded with rivets
  my wardrobe clean

the pick in my hair
  the pomegranate in my hand
14th street   delancey street   103rd street
  reservation where i lay my skull
the barrio of need
  the police state in ashes
drums full of tequila   full of el dorado
  full of banana solitudes say:
Do you really think time speaks english
  in the men's room

UNDER THE EDGE OF FEBRUARY

Under the edge of february
in hawk of a throat
hidden by ravines of sweet oil
by temples of switchblades
beautiful in its sound of fertility
beautiful in its turban of funeral crepe
beautiful in its camouflage of grief
in its solitude of bruises
in its arson of alert

Who will enter its beautiful calligraphy of blood

Its beautiful mask of fish net
mask of hubcaps mask of ice picks mask
of watermelon rinds mask of umbilical cords
changing into a mask of rubber bands
Who will enter this beautiful beautiful mask of
punctured bladders moving with a mask of chapsticks

Compound of Hearts   Compound of Hearts

Where is the lucky number for this shy love
this top-heavy beauty bathed with charcoal water
self-conscious against a mosaic of broken bottles
broken locks   broken pipes   broken
bloods of broken spirits broken through like
broken promises

Landlords   Junkies   Thieves
enthroning themselves in you
they burn up couches they burn down houses
and infuse themselves against memory
every thought
a pavement of old belts

every performance
a ceremonial pickup
how many more orphans   how many more neglected shrines
how many stolen feet   stolen fingers
stolen watchbands of death
in you how many times

Harlem

hidden by ravines of sweet oil
by temples of switchblades
beautiful in your sound of fertility
beautiful in your turban of funeral crepe
beautiful in your camouflage of grief
in your solitude of bruises
in your arson of alert
beautiful

FROM *MOUTH ON PAPER*
(1977)

FOR THE POETS
(CHRISTOPHER OKIGBO & HENRY DUMAS)

I need kai kai   ah
a glass of akpetesie   ah
torn arm of Bessie Smith   ah

the smell of Nsukka   ah
body sweat of a durbar   ah
five tap dancers   ah
those fleshy blues kingdoms from deep south   ah
to belly-roll forward praise
for Christopher Okigbo   ah

I need a canefield of superstitious women   a
fumes and feathers from port of Lobito   a
skull of a mercenary   a
ashes from a Texas lynching   a
the midnight snakes of Damballah   a
liquid from the eyeballs of a leopard   a
sweet oil from the ears of an elder   a
to make a delta praise for the poets   a

On this day approaching me like a mystic
number   oh
in this time slot on death row   oh
in this flesh picking Sahelian zone   oh
in this dynamite dust and dragon blood and liver
cut   oh

I need cockroaches   ah
congo square   ah
a can of skokian   ah
flaming mouth of a howling wolf   ah
the smell of Harlem   ah
spirits from the birthplace of Basuto   ah
mysteries from an Arkansas pyramid   ah

shark's teeth   ah
buffalo   ah
guerrillas in the rainy season   ah
to boogie forward ju ju praise for Henry Dumas   ah

In this day of one hundred surging zanzi bars   oh
In this day of bongo clubs moon cafes and paradise
lounges   oh
In this day's pounded torso of burgundy mush   oh
In this steel cube   in this domino   in this dry
period   oh

I need tongues like coiling pythons   ah
spearheads gushing from gulf of Guinea   ah
the broken ankles of apartheid   ah
to light up this red velvet jungle   ah
i need pink spots from the lips of trumpet
players   ah
the abdominal scars of seven head hunters   ah
a gunslit for electric watermelon seeds   ah
to flash a delta praise for the poets   ah

Because they'll try and shoot us
like they shot Henry Dumas   huh
because we massacre each other
and Christopher Okigbo is dead   uh-huh
because i can't make the best of it   uh-hun
because i'm not a bystander   uh-hun
because mugging is not my profession   uh-unh

I need one more piss-ass night to make a
hurricane   a
i need one more good funky blood pact
to shake forward a delta praise for the poets   a

On this day of living dead Dumas
on this day of living dead Okigbo

I need kai kai   ah   i need durbars   ah
i need canefields   ah   i need feathers   ah
i need ashes   ah   i need eyeballs   ah
i need cockroaches   ah   i need shark's teeth   ah
I need buffalo   ah
i need spirits   ah   i need hurricanes   ah
I need   ah
to make a delta praise for the poets   ah
ah   ah   ah   ah   ah

IN THE MORNING

Disguised in my mouth as a swampland
nailed to my teeth like a rising sun
you come out in the middle of fish-scales
you bleed into gourds wrapped with red ants
you syncopate the air with lungs like screams from yazoo
like X-rated tongues
and nickel-plated fingers of a raw ghost man
and somewhere stripped like a whirlwind
stripped for the shrine room
you sing to me through the side face of a black rooster

In the morning in the morning in the morning
all over my door like a rooster
in the morning in the morning in the morning

And studded in my kidneys like perforated hiccups
inflamed in my ribs like three hoops of thunder through a screw
a star-bent-bolt of quivering colons
you breathe into veiled rays and scented ice holes
you fire the space like a flare of embalmed pigeons
and palpitate with the worms and venom and wailing flanks
and somewhere inside this fever
inside this patinaed pubic and camouflaged slit
stooped forward on fangs
in rear of your face
you shake to me in the full crown of a black rooster

In the morning   in the morning   in the morning

Masquerading in my horn like a river
eclipsed to infantries of dentures of diving spears
you enter broken mirrors through fragmented pipe spit
you pull into a shadow ring of magic jelly
you wear the sacrificial blood of nightfall

you lift the ceiling with my tropical slush dance
you slide and tremble with the reputation of an earthquake
and when i kick through walls
to shine like silver
when i shine like brass through crust in a compound
when i shine shine shine
you wail to me in the drum call of a black rooster

In the morning in the morning in the morning
gonna kill me a rooster
in the morning
early in the morning
way down in the morning
before the sun passes by
in the morning in the morning in the morning

In the morning
when the deep sea goes through a dog's bite
and you spit on the tip of your long knife
In the morning in the morning
when peroxide falls on a bed of broken glass
and the sun rises like a polyester ball of menses
in the morning
gonna firedance in the petro
in the morning
turn loose the blues in the funky jungle
in the morning
I said when you see the morning coming like
a two-headed twister
let it blow let it blow
in the morning in the morning
all swollen up like an ocean in the morning
early in the morning
before the cream dries in the bushes
in the morning

when you hear the rooster cry
cry rooster cry
in the morning in the morning

I said
disguised in my mouth like a swampland
nailed to my teeth like a rising sun
you come out in the middle of fish-scales
you bleed into gourds wrapped with red ants
you syncopate the air with lungs like screams from yazoo
like X-rated tongues
and nickel-plated fingers of a raw ghost man
and somewhere stripped like a whirlwind
stripped for the shrine room
you sing to me through the side face of a black rooster

In the morning   in the morning   in the morning

GIVE ME THE RED ON THE BLACK OF THE BULLET

(For Claude Reece Jr.)

Bring back the life
of Claude Reece Jr.

I want the bullet from his head
to make a Benin bronze
to make an explosion of thunder
to make a cyclone

I want the 14 years of Claude Reece Jr.
shot on the 15th day of september
shot in the back of his head
shot by a police officer in Brooklyn
shot for being black

Give me the black on the red of the bullet
i want to make a tornado
to make an earthquake
to make a fleet of stilts
for the blackness of Claude Reece Jr.
the blackness called dangerous weapon
called resisting arrest
called nigger threat

I want the life of the blackness of Claude Reece Jr.
i want the bullet from his head
to make a protective staff for startled children
to make hooks and studs
for warrior masks

Give me the bullet with the odor
and the smoke and the skin and
the hair of Claude Reece Jr.
i want to make power

to make power for
the blackness of Claude Reece Jr.

the blackness called pent-up frustration
called unidentified negro
called nigger revolutionary

I want the life of the blackness of Claude Reece Jr.
i want the bullet from his head
to make a protective staff for startled children
to make a Benin bronze
to make an explosion of thunder
to make a cyclone
i want the bullet to bring back the blood
of Claude Reece Jr.
i want to make justice

I want to make justice for
the blackness of Claude Reece Jr.
bring back the bullet with the blood of the blackness
of Claude Reece Jr.
i want to make justice
i want to make justice for the blackness of Claude Reece Jr.

SO MANY FEATHERS

You danced a magnetic dance
in your rhinestones and satin banana G-strings
it was you who cut the river
with your pink diamond tongue
did the limbo on your back
straight from the history of southern flames
onto the stage where your body
covered in metallic flint
under black and green feathers strutted
with wings of a vulture paradise on your head
strutted among the birds
until you became terror woman of all feathers
of such terrible beauty
of such fire
such flames
all feathers Josephine
This Josephine
exploding red marble eyes in new york
this Josephine
breaking color bars in miami
this Josephine
mother of orphans
legion of honor
rosette of resistance
this Josephine before
splitting the solidarity of her beautiful feathers

Feather-woman of terror
such feathers so beautiful
Josephine
with your frosted mouth half-open
why split your flamingos
with the white apartheid regime in south africa

Woman with magnificent face of Ife mask
why all the teeth for the white boers in durban south africa
Josephine you had every eyelid in the forest
every feather flying
why give your beaded snake-hips
to the death white boers in durban
Josephine didn't you know about the torture chambers
made of black flesh and feathers
made by the death white boers in durban
Josephine terror-woman of terrible beauty of such feathers
I want to understand why dance
the dance of the honorary white
for the supporters of apartheid in south africa

After all Josephine
I saw you in your turquoise headdress
with royal blue sequins pasted on your lips
your fantastic legs studded with emeralds
as you kicked   as you bumped   as you leaped in the air
then froze
your body breaking lightning in fish net
and Josephine   Josephine
what a night in harlem
what electricity
such trembling
such goose pimples
so many feathers
Josephine
dancer of the magnetic dancers
of the orange flint pelvis of the ruby navel
of the purple throat
of the feet pointing both ways
of feathers now gone
Josephine   Josephine
I remember you rosette of resistance
southern flames

Josephine of the birdheads, ostrich plumes
bananas and sparkling G-strings
Josephine of the double-jointed knees
double-jointed shoulders   double-jointed thighs
double-jointed breasts   double-jointed fingers
double-jointed toes   double-jointed eyeballs
double-jointed hips doubling
into a double squat like a double star into a giant double snake
with the double heartbeats of a young girl
doubling into womanhood
and grinding into an emulsified double spirit
Josephine terror-woman of feathers   i remember
Josephine of such conflicts   i remember
Josephine of such floating   i remember
Josephine of such heights   i remember
Josephine of so many contradictions
of so many transformations   i remember
Josephine
of such beauty
Josephine of such fire
Josephine of such sheen
Josephine of such
feathers i remember you
Josephine   Josephine

OGUN'S FRIEND
(Metal Workshop)

I saw your eyes like bumps of flint
i saw your shoes like high-top boulders
i saw your hands like faces of fire
i saw your fingers like axes of Shango
i saw your body like a rocker of steel

Yo
i heard a hum down there
i heard a rumble down there
i heard a ghost down there
i heard a thunderbolt expel down there
i heard a anvil in the night go hummmmmmmm
down there

Hey whose metals are shouting so loud
they must be the tapper that Ogun knows

whose are those beads so hot and black
they must be brass for Ogun to fill

who's that worker with corrugated gums
it must be the worker that Ogun chose

who's that one with feet like flames
it must be the welder that's Ogun's friend

Yo
i smell a chicken in here
i smell some charcoal in here
i smell a goat in here
i smell some wax in here
i smell a dog in here
i smell some clay and some oil and some blood in here

Hey i see your chains like links of teeth
crowbars
i see your coils like female pouches
barbed wire
i see your grills like braided snakes
fish-net
i see your ladder like a totem of pliers
crocodiles
i see your pipes like razors on tusks
wine bottles
i see your scissors and your keys on the table in there
uh-huhn

Yo
you got pant legs made into hats
you got diamond plates made into walls
you got straightening combs made into steps
you got hammer-heads made into skulls
you got flat-rings made into ears

Pant legs diamond plates
straightening combs hammer-heads
flat-rings
yo

I feel your flux
i feel your sander
i feel your drill bit
i feel your grinder
i feel your drill press
i feel your hack saw
i feel your brick ax

Yo
i saw your windows like sheets of steel

i heard a gong down there
i saw some navels like bushes of wire
i heard a bird down there

Hey
you got lizard tongues made into tongs
i feel your bald spot
you got snakeskins covered in bronze
i feel your chin marks

lizard tongues bald spots
snakeskins chin marks
yo

i smell some fish in here
i see a rail down there
i smell some toes in here
i see a horn down there
i smell some funk in here
i see a knife down there
i smell some ratheads in here
i see a person down there

Who's that one so brown and fine
Ogun's friend
who's that one in green on green
Ogun's friend
who's that one who eats so fast
Ogun's friend
who's that one with toothpaste lips
Ogun's friend
who's that one who spits on tools
Ogun's friend
Yo Ogun's friend

NIGHTTRAINS

When i blow open green bottles
straight across hump of a frozen tongue

when i shove brown glass
through skull of a possum
and pass from my ears a baptism of red piss

when i cry from my butt like a jackal
and throw limbs of a dying mule into the river

when i split venom from the head
burn codeine into a cosmetic paste
and grieve into a wax of dried bulls

when my mystical bunions jam eyes
into searching spit of a starving wolf
into cosmic lips like monkey genitals

And i receive my pickled turned skeleton of rusty chains
in the bodega
i receive a symbolic heart made of five middle fingers
in the bodega
i receive a teeth parade of yellow roses to leave the bodega
and cross the rio grande
onto the flatbed bones of a musty nighttrain

I say
to see me loosen jaws like a snake
to see me exhausted after a few strikes
to see me pay dirt to the ice hog
in my masai-pachuca-doo
squatting on a pillow of old zoot suits
squatting among the names and breeds
breaking down cheeks dotted
on this night train

and i say i dream of the 1943 riots
I say i dream in a hailstorm of riots
And i say riots dream into a mass of skins stooping
on flatbed bones of a funky nighttrain

And when i siphon sweat for fuel
from this patron saint of chronic diarrhea

When i turn this rubber face into a spotted puma
and take on the forceful winds of the prune pickers

When my laughter dominates the last seat
And i burn labor contracts into brown port caca

Then i approach in mother of pearl and human blood
in father of smoking and coughing throats
and in my jelly of coyote strings
who is to say what when i approach

I mean somewhere along the road in this cold cold chicken shit
somewhere along the road in this wasted body
somewhere along the road eat stocks, bonds feathers
somewhere along the road confiscate borders from wild dogs
somewhere along the road shove them into the imperial valley
somewhere along the road cry hard
and let this night train sink its
rundown rectum of electric chairs into heaven
and say fuck it

I see a way through the maroon glass of this milky way
I say i see a way through for the cradle of hulls
sticking through these indigo ankles
I see a way through
for these torn shoes stinking like dead cats
I see a way through for these blood-streaked legs
I say i see a way through
for these pus-riddled holes in their suction-cup lips

and when i pass through toothless combs coming from armpits
of the bodega
when i pass through bats on corkscrews coming
from the bodega
when i push my mortified flesh from this bodega
and walk with the mildew of an old zoot suit
walk tall in my mud-packed-masai-pachuca-doo
walk among the survivors from the musty nighttrains
fuck it
I say dreams are like riots
i say we dream in a hailstorm of riots
and I say riots dream into a mass of skins
coming from flatbed bones of the funky funky nighttrains

FROM *FIRESPITTER*

(1982)

THE RED PEPPER POET

(for Léon Damas)

If you see a cycle of heavy breezes
blowing backward
into massive loops of heat
crossing two oceans after sunset
if you see an avalanche of clouds
pushing forward into jet streams with syncopated thunder
before sunrise
if you see a long stroke of black lightning
flashing in the sky
like a fast flying train
on its way to Savannah at noontime
if you see a medley of slow moving currents
spinning into a hum of furious tornados
at midnight
Tell everybody
The Red Pepper Poet
moving like the eye of a hurricane is going home

Listen to the mud flow into its deep zydeco
the high-speed drills in their tapping shoes
storm flesh flame
ethiopian ash rings
in this luminous hour of potassium bones
with wings like a magma of hot tears
flooding into mouth of the cayenne river

Listen to the shrill evening falsettos
and the filing down of teeth
hatchet dancers carving up shadows
knife men entering with lips of purple-plated chrome
scar tissues opening their pigments
into the 21st century
Boom
Shoot off the guns for this elder

put your hair into the earth
and fill the night with fire ants

Go ahead
and show your respect for this freedom fighter
this great warrior
dangerous orphan
ibeji among ibeji
the Red Pepper Poet with the bull-roarer tongue
Go ahead
shoulder to shoulder
exile to exile
Dance for the Red Pepper Poet who fought so well
so long so many places so many times in
this world of so much suffering
Boni Boni Boni Boni

Won't you dance for this mean banjo player
this dignified volcano
with his hat pushed to one side and his eyebrow up
Won't you dance for the Red Pepper Poet
with the bull-roarer tongue
Go ahead move into the flow of the deep zydecos
into the shrill evening falsettos and the grinding down of teeth
Go ahead and decorate this ground with tobacco leaves
with sea shells with broken bottles
with tiger balm cans with books with wooden daggers
with dollheads with cornshuck
and a tall glass of scotch and soda
Go ahead and let the old-time rhythms roll
for this great pain-carrier poet
who carried his pain into the forest
like earth carries the amazon river
carried his pain
like a sizzling fever carries a hidden jungle
like the sea carries fish glue
and we carry the intensity of these
fragile vaporous magnetic words of revolt between

anthills of ice-covered poverty
and fire coals burning next to iron spikes
on this day mixed in plantango weed
the smell of snake root
rain feathers
rusty nails in solitude of
a smoking typhoon drilling backward
in backwater lashes of hurricane sweat
triple time on stilts across a mardi gras mass
in angles in circles in green paste in purple agua
Zoom

It's the agility of these popping veins
the strong knuckles of endurance
the expanding neck of unpublished flights
that we push together the amber oils up
split into drops one shake
dissect the meaning of the strategy of Damas
arriving on the concourse
the odor of rum and manioc in his hair
Strike up style spellbinder
You had it
and everybody loved the thickness of your accent
the ritual look of fierce crocodiles crossed in your eyes
the secret memories and sacred visions knotted in your smile
the indestructible timing of your spirit
and your natural slashing attitude
Red Pepper Poet with the bull-roarer tongue
Throw off the flames
flame thrower with your dark flesh barrelhouse band come
and blow into our ears now blow

If you hear a solo wind
in sandpaper socks
sanding sounds of superheated stone songs
against sulfurous falling cells on

dry crust dogs
at the pulse of the hawk's scream
at the moment
when fifty drums hemorrhage
in the middle of the rhythms
when the hurricane turns
at the yoke of the curve
among dead spiders
at the end of the choice
when everything drops into your mask
in that position beyond all grief
at that second
this very instant
Won't you dance for the Red Pepper Poet
with the bull-roarer tongue
Go ahead
push your chair forward
and dance for the great warrior poet
who fought so well so long so many places
so many times in this world of so much suffering
Boni Boni Boni Boni Boni

ONCE UPON A ROAD

It was fun
traveling through the heart of this country
just what I needed
enough gasoline
to speed along the highway
in the winter morning
so crisp and white and dirty and cold
my poetry trying to escape the chill
but anyway
it was fun purging the heart of this country
wow
what a beer mug against
mug of a drunk lumberjack on
his way to South Africa
what electricity in mouth of a disco band so full
of the frenzy of nothing
what a great feeling to
look over shoulders of a liberty statue
look up into the oxidized head of
a country so pure in dumbbells
ding dong
what a crowd of Mr. and Mrs. Blank faces going off to war
such a promotion of fear
such fleshless featherless balls
you make me laugh right in the middle of
this fucking poem
and that's not a device to get your attention
once upon a road
there was a country in the heart of
the Crow the Sioux and the Kickapoo

BIG FINE WOMAN FROM RULEVILLE

(For Fannie Lou Hamer)

How to weave your web of medicinal flesh into words
cut the sutures to your circumcised name
make your deformed leg into a symbol of resistance
Big fine woman from Ruleville
great time keeper
and dangerous worker
I use this hour
to eat from your spirit
dance from mouth to mouth with your holler
hold fingers together in remembrance of your sacrifices
And I have chosen to wear your riverstone eyes splashed
with Mississippi blood
and your sharecropper shoes braided with your powerful stomp
and now in your riot stick neck smeared in charcoal burns
and in your bones that exhausted
the god of whiteness in Sunflower County
I will push forward your precious gift of revolutionary courage
Thanks to the southern knife with terracotta teeth
magnificent ancestor
warrior friend
most beautiful sister
I kiss the mud of this moment

NIGERIAN/AMERICAN RELATIONS

They want the oil
But they don't want the people
They want the oil
But they don't want the people
They want the oil
But they don't want the people
They want the oil
But they don't want the people
They want the oil
But they don't want the people
They want the oil
But they don't want the people
They want the oil
But they don't want the people
They want the oil
But they don't want the people
They want the oil
But they don't want the people
They want the oil
But they don't want the people
They want the oil
But they don't want the people
They want the oil
But they don't want the people
They want the oil
But they don't want the people
They want the oil
But they don't want the people
They want the oil
But they don't want the people
They want the oil
But they don't want the people
They want the oil
But they don't want the people

IF THE DRUM IS A WOMAN

why are you pounding your drum into an insane babble
why are you pistol-whipping your drum at dawn
why are you shooting through the head of your drum
and making a drum tragedy of drums
if the drum is a woman
don't abuse your drum   don't abuse your drum
                    don't abuse your drum
I know the night is full of displaced persons
I see skins striped with flames
I know the ugly dispositions of underpaid clerks
they constantly menstruate through the eyes
I know bitterness embedded in flesh
the itching alone can drive you crazy
I know that this is America
and chickens are coming home to roost
on the MX missile
But if the drum is a woman
why are you choking your drum
why are you raping your drum
why are you saying disrespectful things
to your mother drum   your sister drum
your wife drum and your infant daughter drum
If the drum is a woman
then understand your drum
your drum is not docile
your drum is not invisible
your drum is not inferior to you
your drum is a woman
so don't reject your drum
don't try to dominate your drum
don't become weak and cold and desert your drum
don't be forced into the position
as an oppressor of drums
and make a drum tragedy of drums
if the drum is a woman
don't abuse your drum   don't abuse your drum
                    don't abuse your drum

RAPE

What was Inez supposed to do for
the man who declared war on her body
the man who carved a combat zone between her breasts
Was she supposed to lick crabs from his hairy ass
kiss every pimple on his butt
blow hot breath on his big toe
draw back the corners of her vagina and
hee haw like a California burro

This being wartime for Inez
she stood facing the knife
the insults and
her own smell drying on the penis of
the man who raped her

She stood with a rifle in her hand
doing what a defense department will do in times of war
And when the man started grunting and panting and wobbling
forward like
a giant hog
She pumped lead into his three hundred pounds of shaking flesh
Sent it flying to the Virgin of Guadalupe
then celebrated day of the dead rapist punk
and just what the fuck else was she supposed to do

And what was Joanne supposed to do for
the man who declared war on her life
Was she supposed to tongue his encrusted toilet-stool lips
suck the numbers off of his tin badge
choke on his clap trap balls
squeeze on his nub of rotten maggots and
sing god bless America thank you for fucking my life away

This being wartime for Joanne
she did what a defense department will do in times of war

and when the piss-drinking shit-sniffing guard said
I'm gonna make you wish you were dead black bitch come here
Joanne came down with an ice pick in
the swat freak motherfucker's chest
yes in the fat neck of that racist policeman
Joanne did the dance of the ice picks
and once again
from coast to coast
house to house
we celebrated day of the dead rapist punk
and just what the fuck else were we supposed to do

THERE IT IS

My friend
they don't care
if you're an individualist
a leftist   a rightist
a shithead or a snake
They will try to exploit you
absorb you confine you
disconnect you isolate you
or kill you

And you will disappear into your own rage
into your own insanity
into your own poverty
into a word a phrase a slogan a cartoon
and then ashes

The ruling class will tell you that
there is no ruling class
as they organize their liberal supporters into
white supremacist lynch mobs
organize their children into
ku klux klan gangs
organize their police into
killer cops
organize their propaganda into
a device to ossify us with angel dust
preoccupy us with western symbols in
african hair styles
inoculate us with hate
institutionalize us with ignorance
hypnotize us with a monotonous sound designed
to make us evade reality and stomp our lives away
And we are programmed to self-destruct
to fragment
to get buried under covert intelligence operations of
unintelligent committees impulsed toward death
And there it is

The enemies polishing their penises between
oil wells at the pentagon
the bulldozers leaping into demolition dances
the old folks dying of starvation
the informers wearing out shoes looking for crumbs
the life blood of the earth almost dead in
the greedy mouth of imperialism
And my friend
they don't care
if you're an individualist
a leftist a rightist
a shithead or a snake

They will spray you with
a virus of legionnaire's disease
fill your nostrils with
the swine flu of their arrogance
stuff your body into a tampon of
toxic shock syndrome
try to pump all the resources of the world
into their own veins
and fly off into the wild blue yonder to
pollute another planet

And if we don't fight
if we don't resist
if we don't organize and unify and
get the power to control our own lives
Then we will wear
the exaggerated look of captivity
the stylized look of submission
the bizarre look of suicide
the dehumanized look of fear
and the decomposed look of repression
forever and ever and ever
And there it is

FROM *COAGULATIONS*
(1984)

STOCKPILING

stockpiling of frozen trees
        in deep freeze of the earth
stockpiling of dead animals
        in exhaust pipes of supersonic rockets
stockpiling of desiccated plants
        on death root of an abscessed tooth
stockpiling of defoliants
        in pine forest of the skull
stockpiling of aerosols
        in the pink smoke of a human corpse
stockpiling
        of agent orange agent blue agent white acids
        burning like the hot hoof of a racehorse on
                                        the tongue
                                        stockpiling

Look at it
        through antibodies in the body
        through multiple vaccines belching in the
                                                veins
        through cross-infections of viruses
                                        stockpiled
                                        in the mouth
        through benzene vapors shooting
                                into the muscles of the
                                stars
        through gaseous bowels of military
                                fantasies
        through white radiation of delirious
                                dreams
Look
        this stockpile marries that stockpile;
        to mix and release a double stockpile of
                                fissions
exploding
        into shadows of disappearing space

Global incapacitations
Zero
        and boom
This is the nuclear bleach of reality
the inflated thigh of edema
the filthy dampness in scientific pants
                                of a peace prize
the final stockpile of flesh dancing in
terrible whooping cough of the wind
And even if you think you have a shelter
that can survive this stockpiling
                                of communal graves
                                tell me

Where are you going
with the sucked liver of mustard flint
the split breath of hydrogen fumes
the navel pit of invisible clams
the biological lung of human fleas
the carcinogenic bladder of sponges
lips made of keloid scars
memory in numb section of the chromosomes
        Just where do you think you're going
                                with that stockpile of
                                contaminated stink

Listen
When I think of tactical missiles plunging
        into rancid goiters of the sun
The artillery shells of wiretapping snakes hissing and
                                        vomiting
        into depths of a colorless sky
The accumulation of fried phosphoric pus graffitied
        on fragile fierceness of the moon

The pestering warheads of death-wings stockpiling
                                        feathers upon feathers
                                        in the brain
And the mass media's larvae of lies stockpiled
                                        in plasma of the ears
And the stockpiling of foreign sap in fluxes
                                        of the blood
And the stockpiling of shattered spines
                                        in chromium suits
                                                  under
                                                  polyurethane
                                                  sheets
          I look at this stockpiling
at this rotting vegetation
and I make myself understand the target
That's why I say I'm into life
          preservation of life now
          revolutionary change now
before the choking
          before the panic
                    before the penetration
                                        of apathy
                              rises up
                    and spits fire
          into toxic tears
                    of this stockpile

PLAIN TRUTH

They say
jab the pencils
in your tongue
Smash windows
Scream
Holler
Tear up the room
Knock down the books
Hold your mouth open with
a stick
Roll over in a rage
Push your private pain
into a collective sadness &
explode
They want you
to hate yourself
in the fly
of their masturbating teeth
Electrocute yourself
in dryness
of their syntax
Suck
their national standard
of
dead metrical feet
and free-base into
refugee camp
of a make-believe
think-tank
They say
walk with
depressive effects
of
a
toxic

cloud
in
your
skull

Keep that
vaginal
aerosol spray
hissing in
the pussy
Store that
contaminated
fetus
of dioxin in
the womb
Line those lungs
with the snowflakes
of asbestos
and nuke up to see
the glory
of the coming
of the lord
They want you
to be product
consumer
and public authority
all together in one package
without choice
without change
without a human transforming action
Just enter
emulate & exit
Just puke in
pay off
punk out

and
as soon as you receive
the triple internal illumination
of yourself
as a lunatic
just know
it's a direct hit
in
the
head

IN A STREAM OF INK

(Written for the print porfolio produced by the Bob Blackburn Print-Making Workshop)

So many elbows on the bandstand
        so many ideologies grafted together
So many memories coexisting
        so many extensions breaking off
So many scuffles redefined
        so many secretions interlacing
So many whistles hidden in the flesh
        so many exaggerated organs on the horizon
So many tongue-tampering strategies on the
        toothbrush
        so many questions bleeding between dentures
So many uncontrollable punches on the circuit
        so many edges
So many fringes
        so many zones
So many flashpoints plunging
        into rhythm of the moment
                of so much diversity
that even the finest cloth ever stuffed
into the last tremor of a corpse
can become rarest vein in the eyeball of
compression
and robot mucus on the sex pulse of nostalgia
can turn into a nuclear warhead of hot semen
and steel dust on ass of a common pimp
can become a presidential pompadour of acid rain
and the strongest teeth in the grin of humiliation
can become the toothless gums of a fuchsia volcano

Because anything and everything is possible
in this collection of umbilical sweat
bursting forth like a mound of palm leaves
waving into space of the night of assaulted bones
Shapes accumulating like ancestors
in the purple velveteen shadow of leather lungs

A ceremony of rakes and rollers crosshatching
into a gel of artificial light
          Clusters
                    Patterns
                              Infiltrations

The weight of five overlapping facial configurations
split and glued onto a spleen of lingering odors
Textures Contours Colors Juxtapositions
Half lip   half eye   half tones baptizing
in turquoise darkness of a train serenade and
in the center of another slap of epidemic wax
a release   a transfer   an accusation
a corrosion of marks
head units and gyrating limbs parading
in a stream of ink
          Elevations
                    Stilts
A promenading surface of erotic strokes
Rebellions carried on felt tip of an evening sunset
Images
climbing in and out of sensations
in and out of distortions
in and out of the static of chartreuse lightning
With flint and graphite and soot and the knife
          grinders grinding into a paint of pink
          champagne
With smoke and stone and grease and the
magnification
of multiple grooves pressed on a generation of profiles
With bleach and dye and hemp and the metallic
inflammation
          in eyeslit of a sub-zero bump
With volume and theme and
          the spinning suction of Yucatan flames

With flag and map and
dialogical coagulations on mute of a frozen
plate
With lines
contracting   expanding   going deeper
into the damp sound of paper
curving   crossing   shifting   slicing
into quiver of a human impulse
coiling   zig-zagging   swirling
into bite of the process
pushing   piercing   swinging from inner
limitations into outer limits of space   eliminations
in a stream of ink

And it's a collographic jungle of cuts
A photographic blister of red dots
Deformed *cabezas* that are secret wells
Mouth murals of flashing metals
A codex of hidden structures
A refuge for absurd feelings
Gouges
Terrains
Bodies in relief
Bodies absorbed in copper
Bodies subdivided into bodies
Attitudes
Definitions
Dreams
stretching through a labyrinth of shades
Everything intensifying in this
charcoal sandstorming desert
The buzz in the ear
The blow torch blow of barracuda breath
Barbed wire posing on a mask of zinc windows

Apprehensions   Footprints   Invasions
The stench of withdrawal and regeneration
A convulsion of currents   A conduit of
                    confabulations
                    Exhaust pipes of lavender flowers
                                        Impressions
          from coins   from keys   from anthills
          from fifty-five polluted singing winds in a
                                                  stream of

so many calculations
          So many conjunctions
so many uninhibited gestures
          So many toxic runoffs
so many self-inflicted etchings
          So many reef devastations
so many identification stones smoking
          So many tilted forms feathered
so many insertions inserted
          So many conceptions communicated
so many enclosures
          So many events
so many blunted instruments scraping
                    into rhythm of the moment
                                        of so much diversity
                                        in a stream of ink

FROM *SOMEWHERE IN ADVANCE OF NOWHERE* (1996)

ADUPE
(ah doo pway)

1981
& I did not find Nicolás Guillén
but I found Cuba
the Cuba in Nicolás Guillén's poetry
poetry dedicated
to his two selves
his two sides
poetry in half notes
in eighth notes
in 6/8 time
poetry moving backward & forward
like war dances
poetry doing the Rara
in an African vocabulary
poetry of Nicolás Guillén
Nicolás Banjo Guitar Mbira Guillén
improvising like
the great instrument he is
in Yoruba
in Spanish
in Son
not exotic but Zydeco
Not Miami but Havana
not tweet tweet but Mau Mau
Adupe to the man
from Camagüey

This morning I went
into the Paris
of his poetry
& came out with poets
clinking glasses to
Beaujolais Nouveau at Roquet's
I pushed into

Favela of his poetry
and emerged with
carnival costumes
for one-hundred-year
celebration of the
abolition of slavery
I looked through
his blunt poetry
& saw exiles smiling
like rusty bulldozers
& acting like disjointed
chiefs of staff
like broken stags roaming
in everglades of khaki teeth
& clandestine scrotum
I walked through
séance house of his poetry
& came upon fiesta sizzling
in bubble chamber of Aztec clouds
I dived into political content of his poetry
and discovered mysterious caves with
odors of rotting imperialist dust
I looked at shell-lined pelvis of his poetry
and saw infra-green heat of human capacity
snaking down through underground galaxy
of atomic clocks
I moved into
stamina of his poetry & returned
with boxing gloves smelling like
Santería shrines
I ran along the Malecón of his poetry
& found a poverty imbued
with the power to drive straight through
a northern frente frío
I stood in stadium of his staccato yelping poetry

and heard messages coded
& covered with drum heads from Oyó
and I said Adupe Nicolás Guillén
Adupe
for the cavalcade of leaves &
moaning doves & regalia of punching bags
Adupe
for the musky cyclones in bolero jackets
& smoke-filled consultation of yagruma trees
Adupe
for the call & response of collaborating oceans
& the rooster juice splashed on feet
steeped in rumba motivations
Adupe
for the great poetic confrontations
of Nicolás Guillén
Adupe
determination belongs to Guillén
revolutionary thought belongs to Guillén
solidarity belongs to Guillén
Gulla   Efik   Ewe   Fula   Fulani   Twi
belongs to Guillén
Mende   Mandingo   Mossi   Umbundu   Suk
belongs to Guillén
Bomba la conga bomba
belongs to Guillén

Negrismo   Socialismo   belongs to Guillén
completeness of life in poetry
belongs to Guillén
Nicolás   Banjo   Guitar   Mbira   Guillén

digging up roots & making his mark
making his mark
breaking those chains & making his mark
making his mark
mixing up rhythms & making his mark
making his mark
talking to his people & making his mark
making his mark
working with his work & making his mark
making his mark
Nicolás Banjo Guitar Mbira Guillén
Nicolás Banjo Guitar Mbira Guillén
making his mark

DON'T ASK/1980

Don't ask me
who I'm speaking for
who I'm talking to
why I'm doing what I do in
the light of my existence

You rise you spit you brush you drink you
pee you shit you walk you run you work
you eat you belch you sleep you dream &
that's the way it is

In the morning
tap water tastes fishy
coffee sits in its
decaffeinated cup
caca & incense
have a floating romance
& a stale washcloth
will make you smell
doubly stale
so don't get kissed on the cheek
don't get licked on the neck

at 8 a.m.
the trains & buses are
packed with folks farting
their bread & butter farts
the gymnasium
is dominated
by the stench of
hot tennis shoes
& in one locker room
a few silly-talking
intellectual-looking

coke-drinking
cloth-dropping
paper-littering
spinach-pooting
smug arrogant women wait to
be waited on

& in another locker room
there are odors of
crotches & jock straps
bengay, tiger balm
& burning balls
sweat socks & sweat suits
of body-building
door-slamming
iron-pumping
phlegm-hawking men
all sour & steamy
& wrapped up together
in a swamp of
butt-popping towels
but don't let it
get you down
don't let it
psych you up

Outside the ledges are
loaded with pigeons
clouds are seeded with
homeless people &
lyricism of the afternoon
is a sub-proletarian madman
squatting & vomiting
from his bowels
a brown liquid of death
in front of your house

& it's not happening because of you
those socks don't stink because of me
a bureaucrat is not a jerk because of us
I'm not this way because of them
you're not that way because of me
don't ask about influences

You rise you spit you brush you drink you
pee you shit you walk you run you work
you eat you belch you sleep you dream
& that's the way it is

THE MAN WITH ELEPHANTIASIS LEG IN RECIFE, BRAZIL

This leg
oh yes
this leg he said
this leg is
a good-luck charm
a torpedo of fission
a hissing chain that
lays itself down to sleep across
entrances to city markets
oh yes
This leg is
a lipstick-wearing dancer in samba schools
a fat snake that zigzags and
sells poetry pamphlets to strangers before
stall keepers open teeth to yell "guarana"
oh yes
This leg is more than
colonized chapel of parasites
more than any tree of
slashed flesh & calcified sap
This leg is not
just a man-made dam of
filarial worms & feathers erupting through
winter smells of leather
This leg is
the legendary limb that has
an ancient grandfather who
stands in a plaque
on the wall of the British Museum
and a twin sister who
leans against buildings in Chicago
and one cousin who
sits in the shade next to
certain hotels in Egypt

oh yes
this leg
This leg is
a tropical garden
a gas pump
a mountain of sea-foaming blood that
sleeps after midnight
has no football in hell
no bicycle in heaven
but rises like
sweet sausage tongue of the sun
to spit out poems before
the rootmen scrape their barks to holler “guarana”
oh yes
This leg
oh yes

NOW I DIG UP PATINAS

Now I dig up patinas
I chew on slit logs
I polish surfaces of cyclones
I mount bullet wounds to inspect mutilations
I uproot the spirit of
the chemicals that make me
violate myself
I count limited resources
I view sinkholes in
the atmosphere
I lubricate the batás
& provoke in all keys of
flesh & hallucinogenic gongs
the obscenities stuck to
my elbow of whistling bones
& with Olmec sculptors shrieking through
banana grove of my solitude at 12:45 a.m.
& with the jaguars dropping from
my throat
& with the pumice of bulldog ants rising from
my damp discharge zone of
poetic fission
& with medicinal fat of
a big-time rooster
in my nose of talkative boogers
& with torn crows flying from my
brown-bearded ovum of
sulfuric acid blood
& with the insects blowing from
my colon of atomic leaves
& with mescal tears of oppressed fleas
smeared on wings of my ovarian cysts

I detonate
I nuclear react
I frenzy faces of
fascist thought
I become
Zaire River mouth
pissing on every
corrupt officer in an old
leopard-skin Mobutu Sese Seko cap
I unmuzzle my
black stretch-limousine lips
and say
I'm a poet
to vin rouge
vin blanc
drunk fly
corpse of a roach in a cup

THE HEAVY-HEADED DANCE

(For Mel & Ted)

Dancing &
on my head
is the spotted skunk
whose scent did not protect it
from Mr. & Mrs. Archibald of Texas

On my head
is the stuffed bobcat
whose facial expression was set
by the taxidermy department

On my head
is a bull caught
in the act of masturbation
& on top of that
rides the moose
stun-gunned while wading in a lake
& on top of that
are the monkeys
entrapped while urinating
& on top of that
lie the hyena
jackal & vulture
shot while eating from zebra carcasses
& on top of that
sits the ram with the
largest horn on record
donated by Henry Beck

& with all the stuffed animals piled on my head
I am dancing past
lyricist with the baboon heart

I am dancing like a dog
in front of financial consultant
implanted with pig genes

I am dancing & fluttering like a butterfly
across from novelist posing
in a beaver skin coat

I am dancing near the astronomer
who circles the floor with her
uplifted face frozen like a tiger

I am dancing against window
of artificial coyotes
& howling with contemporary African band
in the grizzly bear room

I am dancing my pangolin hairdo dance
past the river of ants in panties
of gyrating vocal groups

I am dancing so many different dances
with so many bloated animals
dead on my head
that my head is
a dancing museum of unnatural history
& I am dancing where I cannot see
myself dancing to know
why I am dancing
but I am dancing
I am dancing

COMPAÑERA
(Ana Mendieta)

Compañera
We should have bolted you down like
a piece of iron sculpture and
pointed you in another direction
but you were busy looking for love
in the wrong dictionary
looking for a sweet papa
in the wrong encyclopedia

& now I say to myself
Ana is dead
not alive
not returning
what would she think of that

She arrived in the Apple
to jog around the park
have lunch with friends
create sculpture
install exhibitions
& get intellectual stimulation from
a drunk lover who swears
he did not throw her
out of the window

Why say
performance artist takes a dive
political thinker leaves in a huff
short intense Cuban shows her anger
big orphan-mouth sculptor leaps

Ana did not leap
because Ana knew
Ana could not fly

So why not say
her breath was filled
with black beans
green tomatoes
mojitos & Guantanamera
with garlic
cerveza
cilantro
the sweet melodies of Beny Moré
River Oshún foam
dark Havana rum splashes
& the water-running rhythms of
Orquesta Aragon

Why not say
She was carver of wood and earth
collector of Cuban jokes
a cyclone in blue tennis shoes
a sequin dress machete
forever cutting through the
dry thunder of oppression
&
it was no dream when she yelled
"that chauvinist shit
that stinking little bitch
that phony bastard with his
fucking elite whores
& his kissing lips full of smoking ass
sucking on this corrupt spirit-breaking system
of fucked-up interventionist agendas"
It was no dream
So why not say
if a short rainbow
signifies in face
of an outbreak of pink marble flames

there will be blood
in hair of the dirt storm
& if respect is a somber silueta
etched in consciousness of a warm cave
there will be an erection of hate
in eurocentric bones
if a conspirator plots
& you cannot overthrow or float
the navel will never know its umbilical future

Why not say
after the exit of two great drummers
& in between the entrance of
one monumental earthquake
a huge volcano eruption
& reappearance of the tail of Halley's Comet
We lost Ana

but Ana did not leap
because Ana knew
Ana could not fly

THESE NEW YORK CITY PIGEONS

These New York City Pigeons
cooing in the air shaft
are responsible for me
stubbing my toe
spraining my ankle
and getting sick on ammonia fumes

That pigeon roosting on the clothesline
stole my nightgown
Those pigeons on the street lamp
made me feel foolish
while riding in a black car
completely splattered
with their grey & white poo poo

These New York City pigeons
are not calm like pigeons of Oxalá in Brazil
and do not croon like doves of Zimbabwe

New York City pigeons moan
strange   low   mournful   quivering cancer-like moans
mixed with
hungry hyena barks
& gulping loss of the forest cries

New York City pigeons
are not relaxed like
pigeons sunning at
Marcel Duchamp swimming pool in San Francisco

New York City pigeons are not happy like
pigeons standing on head of the woman
selling bananas on a street corner in Johannesburg

New York City pigeons
flap viral leather fungus dust from wings into faces
then sit on steps vocalizing & waiting
for the death of humankind

New York City pigeons
are not friendly like
pigeons eating flaky crescent-shaped rolls at
Hôtel du Piémont in Paris

New York City pigeons
are not content
like pigeons
posing for photos on arms
of men in plaza of Caracas

New York City pigeons
will lounge on ledges
& murmur profanity all day
will fight for fucking space in
the mating season
shit on air conditioners
& wipe their asses on windows
while big cockroaches
suck Sucrets in the dark

New York City pigeons
are not alert
like pigeons
sitting quietly on bicycles
in peace memorial park of Hiroshima

New York City pigeons
roll their pearly eyes
inflate their throats
and defecate on the shoulders of pedestrians

New York City pigeons
have no love for crumb-throwing pigeon lovers
& no year of the pigeon is celebrated
at least
not for these New York City Pigeons

GLOBAL INEQUALITIES

Chairperson of the board
is not digging for roots
in the shadows
There's no dying-of-hunger stare
in eyes of
Chief executive officer of petroleum
Somebody else is sinking into
spring freeze of the soil
Somebody else is evaporating
in dry wind of the famine
There's no severe drought
in mouth of
Senior vice president of funding services
No military contractor is sitting
in heat of a disappearing lake
No river is drying up
in kidneys of
a minister of defense
Under-secretary of interior
is not writing distress signals
on toilet walls
Do you see refugee camp cooped up
in head of
Vice president of municipal bonds
There's no food shortage
in belly of
a minister of agriculture
Chief economic advisers are
addicted to diet pills
Banking committee members are
suffering from obesity
Somebody else is sucking on dehydrated nipples
Somebody else is filling up on fly specks
The Bishops are not

forcing themselves to eat bark
The security exchange commission members
are sick from
too many chocolate chip cookies
The treasury secretary
is not going around in circles
looking for grain
There's no desert growing in nose of
Supreme commander of justice
It's somebody else without weight
without blood without land
without a cloud cover of water on the face
It's somebody else
Always somebody else

SACRED TREES

Every time I think about us women
I think about the trees the trees
escaping from an epidemic of lightning
the sacred trees exploding from
compressed matter of cuckoo spit trees
the raped trees flashing signals through
toxic acid of sucking insects
trees used as decoy installations trees

I have the afternoon leaves throbbing
in my nostrils
I have the struggling limbs sprouting from
these ear lobes
I have a power stump shooting from
out of this forehead
I have clusters of twigs popping from
tattooed moles
& sometimes I feel
like the tree trunk
growing numb & dead
from ritual behavior
sometimes I feel like the tree ripping
from the core of ancient grievances
Trees
I feel like
the family tree
relocating under pressure
Trees
I feel like the frantic tree
trying to radiate through
scorched surfaces
sometimes I feel like
the obscure tree

babbling through silver-plated mouth
    of a shrinking moon
& sometimes I feel like a tree
hiccupping through
heated flint of gunpowder crevices
I feel like a tree
& every time I think about us women
I think about the trees
I think about
the subversive trees laden in blood
                    but not bleeding
the rebellious trees encrusted
                    but not cracking
the abused trees wounded
                    but still standing
I think about the proud trees
the trees with beehive tits buzzing
the transparent trees
the trees with quinine breath hovering
the trees swaying & rubbing their
stretch-marked bellies
                    in the rain
the crossroad trees coming from
                    the tree womb
                      of tree seeds
                          Trees
I think about the trees
& sometimes I feel like
a superstitious tree
smelling negative & fragile
                    & full of dislocated sap
I feel like
the tree stampeding from
                    a cadre of earth tremors
I feel like the forgotten tree
          that can't live here no more

sometimes I feel
    like the tree that's growing wild
through the wildlife left
in the petroleum pipeline
                    I feel like a tree
A tree caught
in the catacomb of bones
                    enslaved in
red-light districts of oppression
I feel like a barricade of trees
& sometimes
I feel like the tree
that's lucky to be a tree
          in the time of
              missing trees
I feel like a tree
that's happy to be a tree
among disappearing trees
          Trees
I feel beautiful
          like an undestroyed
          rainforest of trees
I feel like a tree
   laughing in the rawness
             of the wind
I feel like a tree
& every time I think about us women
          I think about the trees
          I think about the trees

THE OPPRESSIONISTS

Art
what do the art
suppressors
care about art
they jump on bandwagons
wallow in press clips
& stink up the planet
with their
pornographic oppression
Art
what do they care about art
they go from being
contemporary baby kissers to
old time corrupt politicians
to self-appointed censorship clerks
who won't support art
but will support war
poverty
lung cancer
racism
colonialism
and toxic sludge
that's their morality
that's their religious conviction
that's their protection of the public
& contribution to family entertainment
what do they care about art

AT A CERTAIN MOMENT IN HISTORY

At a certain moment in history
When Césaire started to decolonize
his neo-colonial head
and free his image
by dealing with the world from
the ideas of Negritude
When young Aimé Césaire said fuck Paree
& returned
to look into the future
by diving inside the past of
                    his native land
When Césaire arrived home to
clarify the contradictions of
too much French wine in
the wee wee of Martinique
When Césaire
who had already incorporated
his multiple rhythms into
the African rhythm section
with Damas & Senghor
When Césaire
who had already exchanged
his clarinet for a drum
began the beguine
in style of Atumpan drummers
& sang until his voice became
the agitated volcano mouth
                    of calamities
It was no exotic voodoo movie script
no get-down-deep-in-the-Congo poetry slam
It was Césaire
          returning to
a forest of dangerous plants
A forest even homeboys didn't enter
without revolutionary intentions

& at that moment of no compromise
his poetry became poetry unique to poetry
his long lava flowing lines moved
beyond classification & geographical links
He fired up words that revolted like
overheated cockroaches
his notebook was the advancement on the path &
sharp point on the spear
He made poetic revolutionary cuts

FROM *THE BEAUTIFUL BOOK*
(2007)

SPOKEN WORD

(Slave Routes Conference: Guadeloupe 12/99)
(For Léopold S. Senghor)

They say within population explosion
there's a spoken word explosion
but there was always a spoken word explosion
exploding on the African continent
& riffing Rift Valley riffs into
throat talking Pharaonic script
that scripted deep Ethiopian cries onto
a circle of eighty spins that became
transformation within
Dogon world inhabited by Hogons
& the spoken word was always the word of words
stacked & ready to erupt from djalis of Gambia
& always word of word in
up-tempo encounters between Khoi and San
between cowrie shells and Ifa priests
Ijala chanters & memory text
between snapping fingers & the poetic tradition of Tiv
Afro field hollers & lamenting dirges of
women in society of Dan
Creole dialects & the click under tongues
double clicking on that
& the word was always the word of words offered as
nasal me now and flatten me out
& flame me like a high-pitched female drum
& patina me in pepper & blood
& speak my dance through the pounding of rice growers
& grow me in low land of the sun
& sun me with Kikongo weavers
& weave me from the spirit of cotton pickers
& cotton me like an ant mound of clans in
the chalky fluid between instincts
& instinct my soul into the magic of burping trees

& tree my luck into falsetto trances
& trance my chaotic laughter back into
syncopated premonitions of how the word
became a proverbial detour of
excavated axe fragments &
invisible crevices within
mathematical equations of
the recyclization of moisture
recolonization of metal
density of edges
& the botanical terrain of bitter-tasting fan belts from
lost paradiddles parading in from Ile-Ife with
the word that was always divided into
bamboo sticks & steel band revolts
& possessed in feathers
& mummified in flint
& expanded by trilling & rolling in with
sharp teeth or shot legs
with rhymes & scratches
with Wolof & Shona
& the horseshoe language of impulse & rupture
& the circumstances left in blown-out throat of a lizard
left under the phonetic hoof of smashed scorpions where the word
was
always the word within population explosion of spoken word
explosions
exploding on the African continent

HAITI 2004

I say Fon   You say Yoruba
I say Bambara   You say Ibibio
I say Ibo   You say Xhosa
I say Kikongo   You say Wolof
I say Fulani   You say BoBo
I say Ashanti   You say Efik
I say Mandingo   You say Mende
I say Luba   You say Lunda
I say Arawak   You say Carib
I say Guinea   You say Dahomey
I say Calabar   You say Zanzibar
I say Angola   You say Senegal
I say Africa   You say Ameri-indian
I say enslavement   You say intense exploitation
I say Marrons   You say invisibles
I say Toussaint   You say Dessalines
I say Christophe   You say Pissed off
I say an amalgamation of languages
You say a pantheon of deities
I say Damballa   You say Legba
I say Erzulie   You say Ogou
I say too many initiations   You say too many superstitions
I say tribalism   You say diversity
I say class rivalry   You say religious infusions
I say soil erosion   You say internal repression
I say lakou de peasant
You say palace elite
I say revolt begins here
You say trouble starts there
Trouble starts with
Who's going be head Negro in the Bantustan
Who's going be chief warlord in the refugee camp
Who's going be top dog on the runway
Who's going be number one drug dealer in the sanctuary
Who's going be the most powerful person

to dominate secrets of the crossroads
Who's going be the most feared killer in
blood ritual of the black code
Who's going be wealthiest mulatto rooster in the cockfight
Who's going be grandest pimp in the temple
Who's going be best prostitute in the national palace
Who's going be the greatest tonton macoute ever lubricated by
the Monroe Doctrine
& who's going be Attaché   & who's going to be Fraphe
& who's going be high on repression
Who's going be possessed into repossession
Who's going to be grinding up leaves all night in
        the British plantation pub
Who's going to be shaking shoulders and slithering down
the trading post in the French bistro
Who's going to be grinning & swallowing zombies all night
        In the US Diplomatic Lounge
I say money be flying   you say violence & poor people dying
I say you say we say Haiti be drinking punishment punch

You say arada
I say petro
You say mambo   I say loa
You say veve   I say ye ye
You say o ke ke   but they say nay nay nay nay
And I say you say we say who they   who they
They be elite-tay they say
They be 3 percent of the population-nay
They say they be Roman Catholics sometime lay lay
They say they economically in charge today day
They town people
They city folk
They big business men
They be chilling in their isolation booth
They be segregated in their thinking
They be delirious devils
They be a Duvalier cult
They be classic Papa fuck-up

They be queen occupation in a marine uniform
They be papa anti-development
They be queen privilege
They be papa devaluation
They be queen bushi dufus ya ya
They be papa CEO of corruption
Be Baby Doc the robot   Be predator Cedras the killer
They be paramilitary brother-hood boo boo cult
They be alienated in their colonial divisions
They be Monsieur and Madame Amnesia living
Their imitation of life in Port-au-Prince

& when I say you say we say Haiti
They say hate it
We say dignity, survival, endurance, consolidation
They say cheap labor, strategic location, intervention
We say justice, education   food, clothing shelter
They say indigenous predatory death squads to the rescue
We say Haitian water violated
Haitian airspace penetrated
They say kiss my aluminum baseball bat
suck my imperial pacifier and lick my rifle butt
We say cancel the debt
They say blow up the green cards
sink all the boat people
We say abolish the military
They say let that coup money march in 2/4 time
We say eradicate poverty, illiteracy, disease, and terror
They say let the celebration for 200 more years of servitude begin
We say viva the Haitian revolution
Viva democracy viva independence viva resistance viva Unity
They say viva the payoff
Viva the rich people viva the widening gap viva regime change
Viva repression
But I say   you say   we say   no way   no way
Haiti be the great symbol of creativity
Haiti be the first to strike blows for independence & culture

Haiti be Samedi sacrifice
Haiti be Baron emergency
Haiti be Vaccine giveaway
Be Gender nomad cooperative
Be chief mineral un-tap-tap
Haiti be Saint grass-root energizer
Be Spell-breaker Wedo
Haiti be Ti-Jean mudslide relief
Be Mystère medicine love ash
Be Daughter lascivious transition
Be agronomist Zo-Bop
Be Da-da-double-face-Boko-hurricane-survivor
Haiti be wanting to be Haiti
Not Haiti bye bye   not Haiti why why
But Haiti independent revolutionary Haiti

& I say Chokwe   You say Fante
I say Hausa   You say Yaka
I say Imbangala   You say Ga
I say Nupe   You say Dinka
I say Soninke   You say Serer
I say Mossi   You say Luba
I say Edo   You say Mandi
I say Zulu   You say Khoi Khoi
I say Swazi   You say Pygmy
I say Baule   You say Masai
I say Dahomey   You say Benin
I say Ga Ga   You say Ra Ra
& I say you say we say Haiti
Come on Haiti   Come on now

FREE TIME FRICTION

(For Ted Joans 2003)

I heard that
A zillion mosquitoes
rode a million human ankles into
the twilight of madness
and even mudfish cults
took off their helmets as
crickets wailing like uncontrollable sirens
lifted you into
baritone fire of the eclipse

and night surfaced with ghosts from Katanga
with lava from city of Goma
with Ouagadougou dust on words
flying on
flying piranhas
back through
crevices of Timbuktu
as you
entered yourself
drinking black stout
chewing kola nut
and riff-raffin like
the great djali you were
with your inflamed spirit lungs
spotted okapi legs
and overheated bongo lips beating in
free-time-friction
very conflictive
very defensive
very Ted-u-nomadically
camel walking forward
& sand-dancing sideways into
a song swallowing its tooth on

a proverb that says:
"The fly has nobody to advise"
& it was
another dawn rising with murmuring roosters
another dump smoking through used wallets
another octopus throbbing between feet of
zoot-suited penguins
another prostate full of untamed windstorms
another ear of canned laughter embedded with
butcher rhythms backed by
horns turning corny lyrics into
beautiful instrumental music
& it was like
another unsanctified shrine chalked in gunpowder
another mask of assertive razors hanging in hallways
another agitated banjo drunk on crocodile tears sold
in plastic bottles to
other civilizations in the mirror of
other planets disappearing with
burros painted like zebras
flamboyant monkeys swinging on
rubber tires in medicine stalls
& the freeze-dried bottom of Mars
re-entering steel-purifying processes in
competition with blowtorch blow of
the trillion trilling tonalities assembled like jackals under
purple postal pulp of your tongue as you yelled
"Tell the Tuaregs I'm on my way"

And it was another pipeline in the treaty
another muted cornet call under
offshore drilling rigs
another bundle of bank notes smiling at
another shitty border dispute
& the battle for who you are
and what you feel
was saying that
"joy is more transient than grief"

& there are
all kinds of uninhabited areas
all sorts of extractions and precipitations
oozing from
sweet surreal marshes of your body splashing into
intersection for irresistible insurrections where
you sit like
an autographed picture that says:
the poet was what he was
and what he was looking for
and deeper than that is not deep
"Tell the Tuaregs I'm on my way"

TALKING ABOUT NEW ORLEANS

Talking about New Orleans
About deforestation & the flood of vodun paraphernalia
the Congo line losing its Congo
the funeral bands losing their funding
the killer winds humming intertribal warfare hums into
two storm-surges
touching down tonguing the ground
three thousand times in a circle of grief
four thousand times on a levee of lips
five thousand times between a fema of fangs
everything fiendish, fetid, funky, swollen, overheated
and splashed with blood & guts & drops of urinated gin
                                        in syncopation with me
riding through on a refrigerator covered with
asphalt chips with pieces of ragtime music charts
torn photo mug shots & pulverized turtle shells from Biloxi
                          me bumping against a million-dollar oil rig
me in a ghost town floating on a river on top of a river
             me with a hundred ton of crab legs
                          and no evacuation plan
me in a battered tree barking & howling with abandoned dogs
my cheeks stained with dried suicide kisses
my isolation rising with a rainbow of human corpse &
                                        fecal rat bones
where is that fire chief in his big hat
where are the fucking pumps
the rescue boats
& the famous coalition of bullhorns calling out names
             hey   I want my red life jacket now
& I need some sacred sandbags
some fix-the-levee-powder
some blood-pressure-support-juice
some get-it-together-dust
some lucky-rooftop-charms &
some magic-helicopter-blades

I'm not prepared
to live on the bottom of the water like Oshun
I don't have a house built on stilts
I can't cross the sea like Olokun
I'm not equipped to walk on water like Marie Laveau
or swim away from a Titanic situation like Mr. Shine
Send in those paddling engineers
I'm inside of my insides
& I need to distinguish
between the nightmare, the mirage,
the dream and the hallucination
Give me statistics
how many residents died while waiting
how many drowned
how many suffocated
how many were dehydrated
how many were separated
how many are missing
how many had babies
and anyway
who's in charge of this confusion
this gulf coast engulfment
this displacement
this superdome shelter
this stench of stank
this demolition order
this crowded convention center chaos
making me crave solitary confinement

Am I on my own
exhausted from fighting racist policies
exhausted from fighting off sex offenders
exhausted from fighting for cots for tents for trailers
for a way out of this anxiety this fear this emptiness
this avoidance this unequal opportunity world of
disappointments accumulating in my undocumented eye
of no return tickets

Is this freedom is this global warming is this the new identity
me riding on a refrigerator through contaminated debris
talking to no one in particular
about a storm that became a hurricane
& a hurricane that got violent and started
eyeballing & whistling & stretching toward
a category three domination that caught me in
          the numbness of my own consciousness
            unprepared, unprotected and
              made more vulnerable to destabilization
by the corporate installation of human greed, human poverty
human invention of racism & human neglect of the environment

I mean even Buddy Bolden came back to say
          move to higher ground
            because a hurricane will not
              rearrange its creativity for you
& the river will meet the ocean in
                    the lake of your flesh again
so move to higher ground
and let your jungle find its new defense
let the smell of your wisdom restore the power of pure air
& let your intoxicated shoreline rumble above & beyond the
water-marks of disaster

I'm speaking of New Orleans of deportation
of belching bulldozers   of poisonous snakes
of bruised bodies   of instability and madness
mechanism of indifference and process of elimination
I'm talking about transformation about death re-entering life with
Bonne chance, bon ton roulé, bonjour & bonne vie in New Orleans, bon

CONVERSATION WITH LANGSTON HUGHES

Someone told TK
And TK told me that
Langston Hughes told them
That he wanted Randy Weston
To play at his funeral the Duke Ellington tune
"Do Nothing Till You Hear From Me"

But every time I hear from Langston
He has too many demands
I mean Langston always
Wants you to talk about rivers
Wants you to be a Revolutionary
Speak in the voice of the people
Dance on some crystal stairs
Listen to Papa Legba on Lenox Avenue
Climb the mountain-top and
Let the Weary Blues echo through your head

You will hear Langston say
Remember the Georgia dusk
Remember the wash-woman
Remember the dust bowl
Remember Mr. Backlash
Remember the Scottsboro boys
Remember the dream number
Remember the bad luck card
Remember the long genealogies
And remember make it black, blunt & beautiful

But when you try to elaborate on that
You will hear Langston say
Development, rhythm, magic
Get off the soapbox
Live and let live
Keep it simple baby Keep it simple

"Do nothing till you hear from me"
If you do nothing till you hear from Langston
And pay no attention to what he says
You'll be working 7 nights a week at
The Elks Club Lounge
& waiting for "Daybreak in Alabama"
While "drying up like a raisin in the sun"

Every time I hear from Langston
He has so many instructions
He wants you
To fill your thoughts full of African folklore
Cha cha cha like a castanet in
District of the Negro
Check out Damballa Wedo
And talk about Louis Armstrong and Patrice Lumumba
In the same breath

And when you say
Langston how can I go from
The "wing tip of a match tip" to the next tip
He'll just say "Ask Your Mama"
And if you start telling him about
The words in your heart reveal
How you feel about him
He'll say that's why his banjo is not sobbing low for you
And hang up the telephone

So if you want to hear from Langston
You will have to know how to
Take the stars out of the sky
Kiss the rain
Deal with the "boogie woogie rumble of a dream deferred"
Suck on the sweet flypaper of life
And Do Nothing Till You Hear From Him
Or you never will

I AM NEW YORK CITY 2

I am New York City 2
It's 9/11/01
& I have been wounded
in the lower Manhattan of my abdomen
Now I am the one with the most wreckage
The most obnoxious smell
& the most industrial volcanic eruption of
twin tower ashes
I am the one flying like an avalanche of
Hazardous waste down the West Side Highway
I carry the gigantic whale of charcoal smoke in
my ground zero head
& everybody will remember me as that
unique contemporary water buffalo dripping pee to
keep fire from burning up the air

I am New York City
Momentarily obsolete, artificial & mad
encrusted, gritty, sober & fuming
but never mind all that
& never mind the profit slump
never mind the central bank
never mind the global financial crisis
never mind those jealous of my cultural dynamism
Forget debate, forget intelligence, forget stupidity, forget it

I have on my hard hat, my gloves, my goggles, my
ear plugs, my gas mask, my welding torch
My tool belt flapping
My tongue clearing the path
My big steel teeth picking up chunks of cement
& I am excavating my ass off

I am New York City 2
& I know who's eating chips in
cockpit of the Federal Reserve
oh yes I know
the stock market crash has not yet fully crashed
but now that the bailouts are bailing out
& the smoke screens are smoking
& the spread of fear is spreading
& the flags are flipping and flying
& the censorship is censoring
& the global crusade is crusading
& the act of terrorism is terrorizing
& now that all the
undermining, mindless, mind-boggling,
mind-controlling freaks are meeting and are taking
mind-blowing missions of destruction to another level
it's time for me
to pump up my muscles
wake up the sleeping birds
make my way through the
transparent maze of insane propaganda
put three hundred pair of
courageous firefighter boots on my head
place a Red Cross sticker on my butt
take a deep breath and
walk in the opposite direction

I am New York City
Always expressive always offensive & always irresistible
So don't play possum with me

THAT CARROT

That carrot
belonging to Brer Rabbit
snatched by Bugs Bunny
then stolen by Bugsy Halliburton
                    & given as
"The Heroic Wartime Achievement Award"
to corporate officers for service
in the oil fields of Iraq
                        now spends
most of its time as
a genetically modified impersonator
impersonating a real carrot
& struggling to keep its color while
fighting to win a popularity contest among
auditors, contractors, farmers & other expert embalmers

OKRA

In that frenzied period
just before entering into
the center of possession
Okra has sex with itself
& even though
most people refer to its potent slime as snot
this infiltrator &
inventor of secret paths
this passionate vibrato singer
& producer of the great soup kanjia
is still celebrated as
the main connector between visible
& invisible forces

CHEESE

In the process
of the process of the process
Cheese
with no bones
& no ancestors
escaped from a monastery
became a leisure-class citizen in northern retreats
a great hit at wine-tasting festivals
& life of the party
in New York, Paris &
San Francisco art world promo events
This milky evangelist
known as the original meltdown
is now
the wildest growing infection
in the Western Hemisphere

WHAT A MOUTHFULL

TOMATO

The tomato
emulates itself
& takes up citizenship
in the garden where
death accepts death

AVOCADO

An avocado seed
sits on
a mound of fish bones
& discovers modern art

KOLA NUT

The kola nut
gets high
on its own bitterness

EGGPLANT

An eggplant cannot really be
what it is said to be
because it is not a capital city in
the great peninsula of palm oil

ON THE JOB IN 2000

A new century
& even the Pope
out of ideas
hungry for publicity
gets into the act
by saying
I bought me some big lips
frizzled up these few strands of hair
tilted my beanie
& now I got the blues

INTEGRATION

I knew the Father
the Son   the Holy Ghost
Ave Maria   Hail Mary
Dalai Lama   Mother Teresa   the Virgin of Guadalupe
Father Divine   Brother Moses
Daddy Grace   Sister Ruth   Queen Mother Brown
Jimmy Swaggart   Aimee McPherson
Rev. Wright   Rev. Moon
Mr. Judas   Mr. Buddha
Mr. Muhammad   Queen Elizabeth   & the Pope
We all went to Gompers Junior High School

BALLROOM AUDUBON

Ballroom Audubon
that's me
I don't have to sit still
I don't have to wait for corroboration
my tables are blessed
with the exaggerated teeth marks of
players & dancers
circling & swinging chairs
in search of spiritual intervention
& yes I have dust from a million encounters
my walls have tobacco stains, green reefer grime
black cherry lipstick smears
nut brown face powder sweat
royal crown hair pomade dots, coco chanel toilet water splashes
& little specks of smack
that's a fact
why not
the secrets in this world
belong to me
I'm the delivery room for new organizations
& the cancellation hall for irrelevant ideologies
listen up
if the Solomon Islands
are being swallowed by the ocean
people from there will just have to
come on home to Harlem
& I'll be waiting in uptown Manhattan
with my cultural lifeline
my primary school for psychological headaches
& my emergency exit for flirting lovers &
violent showdowns
Yes, yes
I party with all parties
chant with all chanters
concert with all concert goers and

collaborate with famous faith healers
funeral directors newscasters beauticians preachers
& political activists
check it out
I'm listed in the dictionary of who's who
and I have spots made by ingredients
of every cleanser known in the universe
can you believe it
I carry fingerprints of each person
that ever touched this microphone
& my floorboards are matted with split reeds
sealed with the strong-smelling resin of
grieving widows
embedded with
shouts & screams &
the scrambling footsteps of an audience
betrayed by someone
we once called beloved
you hear what I'm saying
it was a nasty fonky day
a day dominated by
self-hatred & the misplaced loyalty of
negro killer convicts
sent on a suicide mission
to blow holes through
the X of my Malcolm
& now
frozen in that blood
I am Ballroom Audubon
sweet-smelling birthplace of a martyr

SHORT POEM / LONG STORY

Without négritude
there would be
no métissage

COUP

If your coup
don't come through
then exile
with a smile

HISTORY

Dear Friends
I am not talking about
the black writer and
his white literary father
i'm talking about
black music opposed to
enslavement & colonialism
yes jazz has a color
without that fact
there is no jazz

DEFINITIONS

Democracy is a word
made up by
dispossessed porcupines
in the rectum of another word
called modernity
that's why
when it comes to puffing cigarettes
the masses are uncontrollable

IMPERIAL HIGHWAY

What you think can put you in jail
  what you say may be used against you
    whatever you do to protect yourself will be
      seen as a strike against the patriot act which
        will strike you down for being patriotic to yourself

TELL IT TO ME
NOTES IN ETHIOPIA

Is the Blue Nile blue enough
is Lake Tana fully tainted
are you draped in long white cloth
to beat drums in dampness of
this monastery because
you are the monk
with a Thelonious Monk face
acting impassive & in solitude
as guardian of a building where you stand in doorways
rocking & gonging to announce another sunset
are you the rainbow specialist in this rainforest of
mummies & candles
is that you lying on stone protrusions
humming like a hive of frantic bees then
stepping on toes in border feuds
can this be you
traveling in dryness of a climate change
no longer nomadic enough to be nomadic
but just superstitious enough to be
supernaturally religious
& how many times will you ask me
to take off my shoes before entering into
the swollen military eyes of your frescos
& how fanatical should I be to reach
the fossilized remains of Lucy
are you the make-believe moon in
my horn of Africa marking time while
saying to your fingers "I'm a monk"

tell it to me Ethiopia
because
I am that woman
walking up hills
with stacks of wood on shoulders

the women picking splinters from hands
& pressing cheeks against church walls
asking for another kind of existence
that's me
sucking on stones
whispering to saints
& riding burros down mountainous roads while
living & aging & carrying spirits of dementia to
millennium sunday celebrations
in hooray of the plaza for
long-distance runners
            So tell it to me again
because everybody is singing & saying
something about Queen of Sheba
metal crosses of Axum
Ark of the Covenant
plateau of doves
parade of obelisks
bare feet on rough surfaces
airplane turning around in mid-flight
but what is the turn around motion
in the lord have mercy on my soul in Gondar
where you sit
on edge
of my imagination
shouting that
you are Lalibela too
a city which you stuff in my nose
a stone quarry of churches
invented indented
& inverted by rebellious angels
which you stamp on my forehead

and when I step into
precipitation of your chipped cavity
& scratch on your concrete incisions
looking for spiritual revolts
I feel your volcanic activity
I smell your uprooted debris
I bury my words
deep inside your trench of red lava
for I am in the romance of this collaboration
without experimentations
without scientific explanations
without being in a state of possession
& I know that you are
owner of the dust to dust
leader of the time after time
& tongue of the stand-by-me cries of civilizations
so tell it to me again
because I have put everything on hold to
write my name
on rear end of the donkey
but that ass
already branded with a cross
is praying
"please make me invisible to humans"

DISASTER

A hundred rebels stinking together
in ethnic rage
religious fanaticism
xenophobic meanness
    high on bloods
    & crips
    & renamo
    & the ghost of Mobutu
    Janjaweed
    the lord's resistance army
    & the spirit of Tshombe
    showing up with the face of Morgan
                    in Zimbabwe
Now
South African township lyrics turning nasty
            brother man
            thug angel
            warlord
            schoolboy
            with pack on back
becoming unemployed youth
with hammer, machete & stick
rampaging and
acting independently vicious
economically desperate
politically unproductive
spinning out of control
flooding erupting
& becoming
a natural disaster

IN THE CROSSWALK

Me
I'm just a pedestrian in the crosswalk
& I can't have a nice day in the dioxin
I can't have a great night in the radon
I can't have a fantastic time
listening to voice of a born-again warlord urging folks to
blast nations off the globe
& bang flesh into chemicals

I'm not thrilled by scenes of human destruction
I'm not fascinated by weapons of mass devastation
I'm not in a blow-up-the-planet cult
& ready to ride shrapnel into zero gravity of space

I'm just a pedestrian in the crosswalk

I may not be able to outrun a cheetah
or protect myself against a grizzly bear without hardware
But I can use my brain to explain
why being lifted into a future of unlimited promise by
sixty billion tons of TNT is not for me even though
I'm just a pedestrian in the crosswalk
yes just a pedestrian in the crosswalk

STATES OF MOTION 2

The Afro beat man strutted into himself
with a fabulous shrine of
musical instruments on his head
& the palm wine drinkard danced
into the bush of ghosts with
feather woman of the jungle
while the journalist from Chelsea
entered his time capsule
& the great poet from Chicago
put her latest poem between her lips
and climbed into her baobab tree
& a playwright who departed Congo-Brazzaville
left in a theatre made of whirlwinds
a rare book dealer buried in cigarette butts & ashes
became the first university place bookshop ghost to
inhabit the NYU Library
Bob Rogers the great Afro-American designer returned to the sky
as a shining star when
he lifted off the planet in his total tote bag made of red canvas &
royal blue cotton from Oaxaca
& when Horace Tapscott heard Taps
he rode his piano through the aftermath
& when Carmencita Romero became a moving light leaping into
the tropical evening on board a luxury liner headed for Japan
Pancho Mora Sr. was seen traveling back & forth on a boat made
of wild roses
& as Lynell Hemphill stood in the exit looking for Julius who had already
crossed the ocean to join a bogolan collective in Segu
Tom Feelings was spotted in
the middle passage of his drawings
& Mas Tandine was called upon to create
architecture for an invisible town in Senegal
Francisco Romão de Oliveira e Silva
rejuvenated himself & orchestrated his return to Luanda
then Emilio Cruz ambled from the wilderness with
a magnificent series of paintings and manuscripts

Al Loving wrapped his body in one hundred painted canvas strips &
set off for the egungun festival
John Hicks packed up his piano keys and
took the greyhound bus back to St. Louis
Hilton Ruiz entered the other world like a newborn baby
Alberto Chissano left Maputo wearing
a mask painted with a face resembling Amos Milburn
Leon Golub made his last call at 12 a.m.
Rudolph Baranik stepped out to investigate
the full moon in Pluto
Alice Coltrane hurried off to reminisce with
John about ascensions
Jackie McLean stored his saxophone in the
sanctuary and went to watch the sunrise in Harlem
Bodie sent for Raymond
& after blowing reefer smoke on
the secret poetry society of America
Pedro Pietri put on his applejack cap
& tuxedo t-shirt
then sailed off in an antique telephone booth
to have an extended conversation
with himself in tuxedo junction
& the television journalist from New York
the storyteller from Dakar
the Filipino artist from New Jersey
the pearl diver from Manila
the sergeant from Arkansas
the motorcyclist from Compton
the blues singer from Mississippi
the novelist from lower Eastsida
the children from Casamance
the elders in the storm of Katrina
the tenor player from Memphis
the alto player from Brooklyn
the sculptor from Louisiana
the Trinidadian organizer from London
the clarinetist from Baton Rouge
the poet from Houston
the gambler from Los Angeles

the swimming aunt from San Diego
the duo from Alexandria
& the famous actor from North Carolina
all waited in the forest for Billy Higgins & other drummers to arrive
with conga player Tata Güines of Cuba
meanwhile June Jordan marched away and returned like
a good little soldier in June
Andrew Hill left the crowd to cast a spell on the hilltop
Leroy Jenkins buried his violin at the end of a roadless road
& disappeared
Barbara Ann Teer sent her spirit back to Nigeria
Nellie Lutcher went through the mist looking for Sid Catlett
Judy Simmons locked herself in Club Alabam to concentrate on poetry
Vincent Smith paddled away in a canoe full of art supplies
Dakota left her voice on Broadway
Charles "Diddy" Moffett the optimistic teacher with the legendary smile
shoved off for the banana pudding festival
Benny Andrews pushed his work to significance then
boarded the afternoon train to Georgia
Octavia Butler became a science fiction teacher on Jupiter
Ousmane Sembene taped his battle scars to his camera
put on his everyday cap   puffed on his pipe   & took his cinematic self
into the other world market as
St. Clair Bourne made his entrance in a new documentary
Sekou went searching for Sundiata
Eleo danced his way back to Colombia
Max Roach crossed meters, kept time & m'boomed until
Aimé Césaire carried his volcano of flint & mug of revolt
into the negritude complex
then everyone came from all directions
going to Texas   going to Tulsa   coming from Havana
staying in Toronto   never leaving Benin City
flying south to singsong with song birds
going west to peacock with peacocks
whistling to each other
& enjoying transformation with
a pantheon of bass players
at the gin libation parties

WHAT A MOUTHFULL

Tradition
Emotion
Flamboyant gas leaks
Volcanic fumes
Geography
Landfills
Refuse
Dry spell
& Saint Archaeology
It's you
with that bandit cyclone
actively
dissing the sun
for drinking too much
insecticide
Importation
Invasion
the climaxing battlefield
beneath the earth where
the origin of language
sinks back into
afterbirth
And now visions are batons
dreams are diviners
implications are sunspots
The sky is a toaster
& my dear
you are not the transformer
not the generator
not the transmission
not the axle
You are the copy machine
& at the moment
Mr. & Ms. Photostat
life is saying

let's have a riot in the reproduction room
and on the way to the drunk tank
let's fall on our teeth then meet again
behind mirror on the ceiling of the navel of a new star
and innovate
let's strum in like banjos & koras
& shine like dark rum bottles in bolero jackets
let's return from the other world of saturated tools &
celebrate
like clamoring marimbas
like hallucinating xylophones
& balaphonic gourds
Oh what a mouthfull of
transparent fisheries & inflamed forests
manifestations & manifestos
mutations & erosions
metaphors & validations
Oh what a mouthfull
what a mouthfull

I WAS DREAMING

I was dreaming when I heard a pigeon saying:
If I told you I flew to the moon
I flew to the moon
now I'm back and energized
but I don't eat leftover crumbs anymore
& if I keep watching you chew
I may lose my shadow
Of course I wear my own feathers
and will not disguise my vocals each morning when I perch on your
                    window sill repeating my cru cru call
no matter how many times you hit the glass
or how much vinegar you try pouring on my face
I talk the talk of a pigeon
I crap on umbrellas in the rain before umbrella ladies
          start their violent umbrella attacks
I smell like a pigeon   I walk like a pigeon
I don't have to have an imagination
I know how to hold my head high
                    bend my neck low
          spread my wings and fly
but if I had to be like you
& sing "summer time" every time I opened my mouth to sing
          I'd go crazy
However I'm not in the mood to adjust your blood pressure
so I'm going to sit on my favorite limb and let the sun honk while i
                                                            coo coo coo coo coo